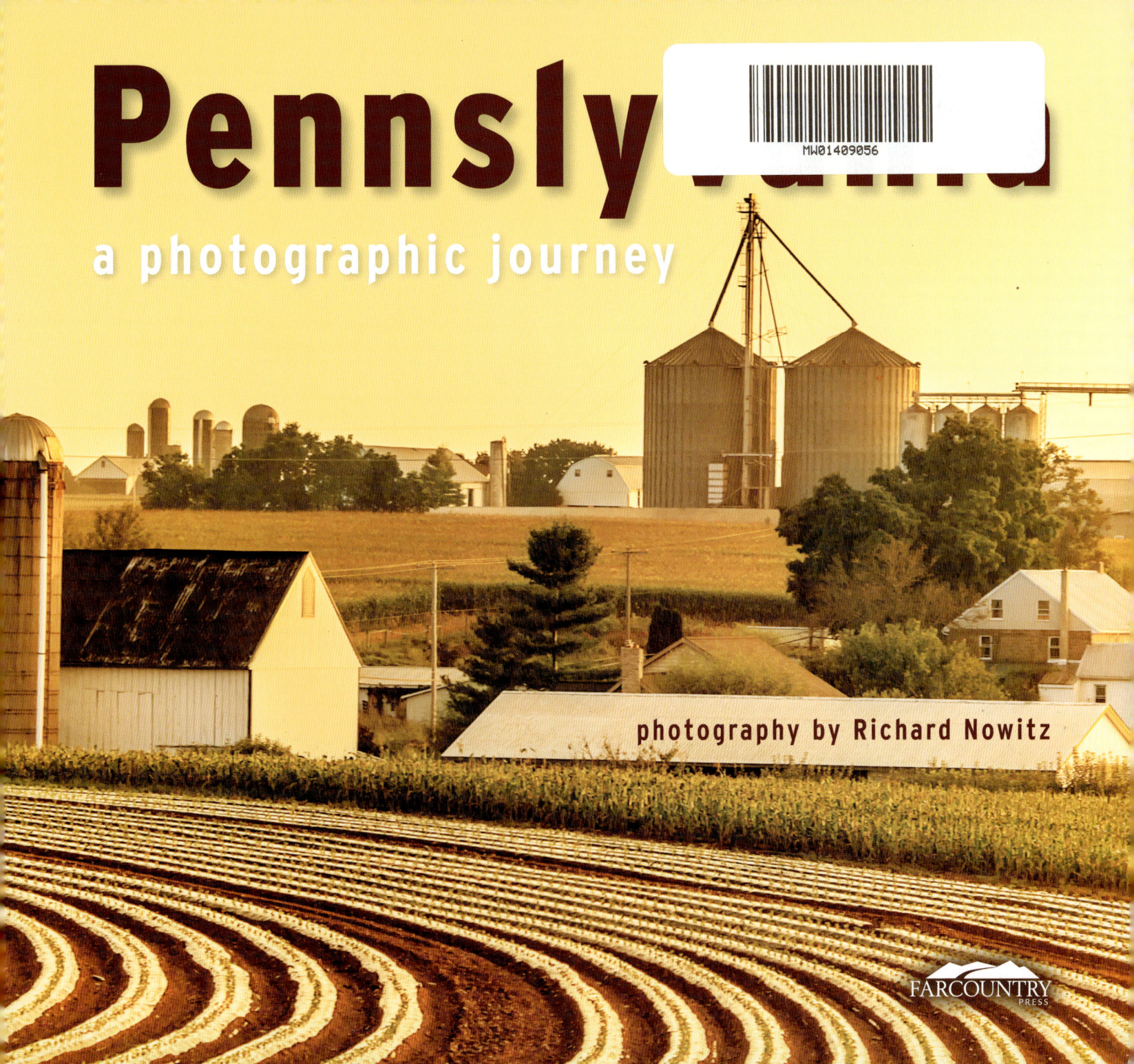

# Pennslyvania
## a photographic journey

photography by Richard Nowitz

FARCOUNTRY PRESS

*Right:* Dedicated on July 4, 1874, the forty-three-foot Soldiers and Sailors Monument keeps watch over Penn Square in downtown Lancaster.

*Far right:* Visitors to Valley Forge National Historical Park can tour the Isaac Potts House, which served as General George Washington's headquarters during the Continental Army's 1777–78 winter encampment.

*Title page:* Farmlands cultivated by Amish and Mennonite families provide a scenic backdrop along Route 23 in eastern Lancaster County.

*Front cover:* Fall colors on the rolling slopes of the Allegheny Mountains complement the greens and reds of a brick farmstead. The farmhouse stands on the grounds of Frank Lloyd Wright-designed home Kentuck Knob in Dunbar.

*Back cover:* Proud symbols of American freedom, the Liberty Bell and Independence Hall stand just a stone's throw apart in Philadelphia's Independence National Historical Park.

ISBN: 978-1-56037-592-0

© 2015 by Farcountry Press
Photography © 2015 by Richard Nowitz

All rights reserved. This book may not be reproduced in whole or in part by any means (with the exception of short quotes for the purpose of review) without the permission of the publisher.

For more information about our books, write Farcountry Press, P.O. Box 5630, Helena, MT 59604; call (800) 821-3874; or visit www.farcountrypress.com.

Produced in the United States of America.
Printed in China.

19 18 17 16 15    1 2 3 4 5 6

*Above:* The central tower of PPG Place, a gleaming complex of buildings in the heart of downtown Pittsburgh, soars over the shops of historic Market Square.

*Right:* Observers take in spectacular views of Pittsburgh's skyline from the upper station of the Duquesne Incline on Mt. Washington. Opened in 1877, the cable car is one of the few remaining cable or funicular railways in the country, and one of two in Pittsburgh.

*Far right:* Benches along the Schuylkill River provide a sunset view of Philadelphia's skyline.

*Right:* A Ben Franklin look-alike leads tours around Old City Philadelphia.

*Below:* Robert Indiana's pop art steel statue *LOVE*, a beloved symbol of the City of Brotherly Love, draws visitors to John F. Kennedy Plaza near Philadelphia's City Hall.

*Far left:* Once a bustling passenger train station, the Radisson Lackawanna Station Hotel now operates as a full-service inn near Steamtown National Historic Site in Scranton. The six-story neoclassical landmark opened in 1908 and features a Tiffany stained-glass ceiling, Italian and Austrian marble, and terrazzo floors.

*Left:* The railroad industry propelled Pennsylvania to the forefront of mining and factory production with a reliable, cheap form of transportation. Steamtown National Historic Site in Scranton showcases rail travel's heyday with interactive exhibits and restored locomotives, train cars, and other artifacts.

*Below:* A restored caboose from the Lehigh & New England Railroad sits at Steamtown National Historic Site.

*Far right:* With the Philadelphia Museum of Art in the background, twilight arrives at the Swann Memorial Fountain in Logan Circle. Designed by Alexander Stirling Calder as a paean to the city's major waterways, the fountain and its surroundings are a place of leisure for Philadelphians and tourists visiting Benjamin Franklin Parkway attractions.

*Right:* Opened in 1815 as the nation's first major urban water supply system, the Fairmount Water Works is a National Historic Landmark and now operates as an education center along Philadelphia's Boathouse Row.

*Below:* Today, more than 1,300 animals reside in America's oldest zoological park, the Philadelphia Zoo, which opened its gates in 1874.

**Far left:** Part of a steel manufacturing tradition dating back to 1857, Bethlehem Steel's decommissioned blast furnaces have a new purpose as a backdrop for free outdoor concerts staged every summer by Levitt Pavilion at the SteelStacks arts complex.

**Left:** The historic Bucks County Playhouse in New Hope stages musicals and plays in a former gristmill on the banks of the Delaware River. Grace Kelly, Lillian Gish, Dick Van Dyke, Robert Redford, and many other stars have performed here since the theater first opened in 1939.

**Below:** Built on former Bethlehem Steel property, the Sands Casino Resort is one of the state's busiest gaming complexes.

13

**Above:** According to lore, George Washington did not sleep at the Black Bass Hotel in Lumberville. When he came looking for a room, the inn was a Tory outpost loyal to the British Crown and not inclined to take in the Commander-in-Chief of the Continental Army. However, its restored riverfront rooms and restaurant draw many modern-day Americans.

**Above, top:** The steel-truss New Hope–Lambertville Toll-Supported Bridge carries pedestrians and cars between the Delaware River towns of New Hope, Pennsylvania, and Lambertville, New Jersey. It was built in 1904 to replace a wooden covered bridge destroyed by flooding.

**Left:** Enjoy exquisitely arranged flora, fountains, and Victorian conservatories year-round at Longwood Gardens.

*Above:* Sweet aromas and street lamps shaped like Hershey's Kisses accent Chocolate Avenue, the main thoroughfare in Hershey.

*Left and above, top:* Opened in 1907 as picnic grounds for the employees of Milton Hershey's chocolate factory, Hersheypark now features more than sixty-five rides, including twelve rollercoasters and a wooden carousel.

*Facing page:* A fountain and tiled floors grace the lobby of the Hotel Hershey, a palatial Mediterranean-style edifice built by Milton Hershey in the 1930s.

*Far left:* Fall foliage frames the Youghiogheny River near Ohiopyle State Park in western Pennsylvania.

*Left:* The Strasburg Railroad, showing off 1830s-era, coal-powered steam locomotives, offers rides through the Amish countryside 365 days a year.

***Below:*** Two tenant houses, a covered bridge, and a restored iron master's mansion are part of historic Poole Forge, an "iron plantation," or self-sufficient iron-producing community, perched along Conestoga Creek. It was one of a string of iron forges operating in northern Lancaster County and vicinity in the eighteenth century.

*Above:* Visitors can get a feel for sea life at the ocean touch tank in Allentown's Da Vinci Science Center.

*Left:* Art and gardening merge in a former vacant lot on Pittsburgh's North Side. Known as Randyland, the site was transformed into a vibrant feel-good oasis by Randy Gilson, a local waiter who wanted to showcase the city's artistic side.

*Far left:* Hundreds of water lilies stretch across the ponds in front of the expansive conservatory at Longwood Gardens in Kennett Square. Begun as an arboretum in 1798, the gardens continue the artistic vision of Pierre S. du Pont, who saved the grounds from destruction in 1906.

***Facing page:*** Rowing on the Schuylkill River by Boathouse Row is a proud tradition that began in the nineteenth century. The growth of the sport helped turn Philadelphia into a major center for rowing and regatta events.

***Below, left:*** Pennsylvania's scenic mountains and forests provide ample opportunities to appreciate nature.

***Below, right:*** A stroll among ornate Victorian homes reveals Pittsburgh's beautiful North Side, one of the city's oldest neighborhoods.

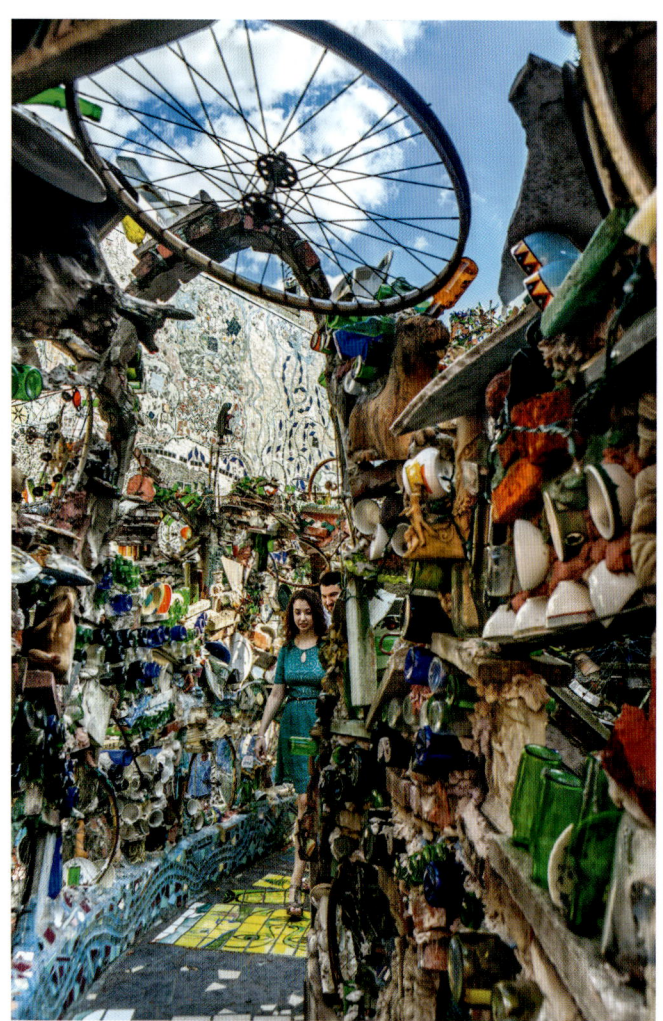

*Above:* Hex signs, a form of Pennsylvania Dutch art, adorn many centuries-old barns in the southeastern corner of the state.

*Left to right:* Just outside of Schellsburg, an eighteen-foot Pied Piper toots to drivers along the Lincoln Highway, the first transcontinental automobile road.

In 1994, artist Isaiah Zagar began tiling a vacant lot in Philadelphia with discarded glass and porcelain—and hasn't stopped yet. The half-block complex known as Magic Gardens on South Street is open for tours and folk-art workshops.

High-spirited, banjo-strumming Mummers strut down city streets every New Year's Day, a Philadelphia tradition dating back to the 1600s. Their extravagant costumes and colorful history are on display year-round at the Mummers Museum in South Philadelphia.

25

***Above:*** The eleven-foot-high Robert Berks bronze statue of children's television icon Fred Rogers, a Pittsburgh native, faces the double-decker Fort Pitt bridge on the Monongahela River.

***Right:*** A cyclist navigates the Three Rivers Heritage Trail in Pittsburgh.

***Facing page:*** The Cathedral of Learning on the University of Pittsburgh campus houses offices, libraries, a computer lab, a theater, and exquisite nationality-themed classrooms. Its forty-two stories make this Gothic revival tower one of the tallest educational buildings in the world.

**Above:** The cheesesteak—thinly sliced sautéed rib eye beef and melted cheese on a long roll—is a Philadelphia institution. The cheesesteak above comes from Pat's King of Steaks, founded by the sandwich's original maker, Pat Olivieri.

**Right:** At the intersection of 9th Street and Passyunk Avenue in South Philly, Pat's King of Steaks and Geno's Steaks have faced off for more than forty years over who makes the best cheesesteak sandwich.

*Far right:* Perched on a hilltop outside Pittsburgh, Fort Ligonier is an eighteenth-century British fortress and the site of a key battle in 1758 during the French and Indian War.

*Right:* A thirteen-star flag on a Lambertville home shows off the Keystone State's colonial heritage.

*Below:* Mourners leave mementos in honor of the fallen at Flight 93 National Memorial. The site of hijacked United Airlines Flight 93's September 11, 2001, crash lies between the towns of Somerset and Shanksville.

**Above and facing page:** David Lynch studied here, as did Mary Cassatt, Thomas Eakins, and Maxfield Parrish. The Pennsylvania Academy of the Fine Arts on Broad Street in Philadelphia is housed in a Victorian Gothic building that served as the nation's first art museum and school. It boasts an impressive collection of American paintings and sculptures.

**Above right:** The Greco-Roman facade of the Philadelphia Museum of Art's Main Building faces the Benjamin Franklin Parkway. One of the country's largest art museums, the institution is home to hundreds of thousands of artworks, including important collections of Asian, European, and American art, and the famous "Rocky Steps," which fictional boxer Rocky Balboa scales in five Rocky films.

*Above:* The world's oldest steel warship still afloat, the 344-foot cruiser USS *Olympia* is docked outside the Independence Seaport Museum at Penn's Landing in Philadelphia. Launched in 1892 and decommissioned in 1922, she is the only surviving naval ship of the Spanish-American War. Her last mission was to carry the Unknown Soldier from France for interment in the United States in 1921.

*Right:* Technology has advanced since the nation's first mint struck its first coins in 1792. Today, the public may watch the Philadelphia U.S. Mint manufacture circulating coins at a rate of 2 million per hour.

*Far right:* Philadelphia City Hall, built at the turn of the nineteenth century and larger than the U.S. Capitol, remains a striking structure in the city skyline. A thirty-seven-foot statue of city founder William Penn stands at the top.

*Facing page:* An architectural masterpiece of cantilevered terraces and waterfall views, Fallingwater, in Bear Run, was designed by Frank Lloyd Wright in the 1930s for the Pittsburgh businessman Edgar Kaufmann. Located in southwestern Pennsylvania's Laurel Highlands, it is the only intact major Wright-designed house open to the public.

*Left:* The tusk of a mastodon serves as the railing for the spiral staircase in the whimsical studio and home of Wharton Esherick, a pioneer of the Arts and Crafts movement who settled in Paoli near Valley Forge.

*Below:* The Kuerner Farm in Chadds Ford was an important source of inspiration for influential painter Andrew Wyeth, who grew up nearby. Today the farm is part of the Brandywine River Museum of Art, which celebrates the artistic achievements of Wyeth and his family.

**Facing page:** History buffs and curious civilians turn out every summer to reenact the Civil War's bloodiest engagement, the three-day Battle of Gettysburg, which claimed the lives of as many as 51,000 soldiers.

**Right:** A gallant soldier dashes into action atop the First Minnesota Volunteer Infantry Regiment Memorial, one of 1,320 monuments and memorials scattered across Gettysburg Battlefield. Behind it rises the largest such monument, the State of Pennsylvania Memorial.

**Below:** Sprawled across nearly 6,000 acres, Gettysburg National Military Park preserves 48 historic buildings and a few hundred cannons. This bronze cannon accompanies a monument to Battery E of the 1st Rhode Island Light Artillery.

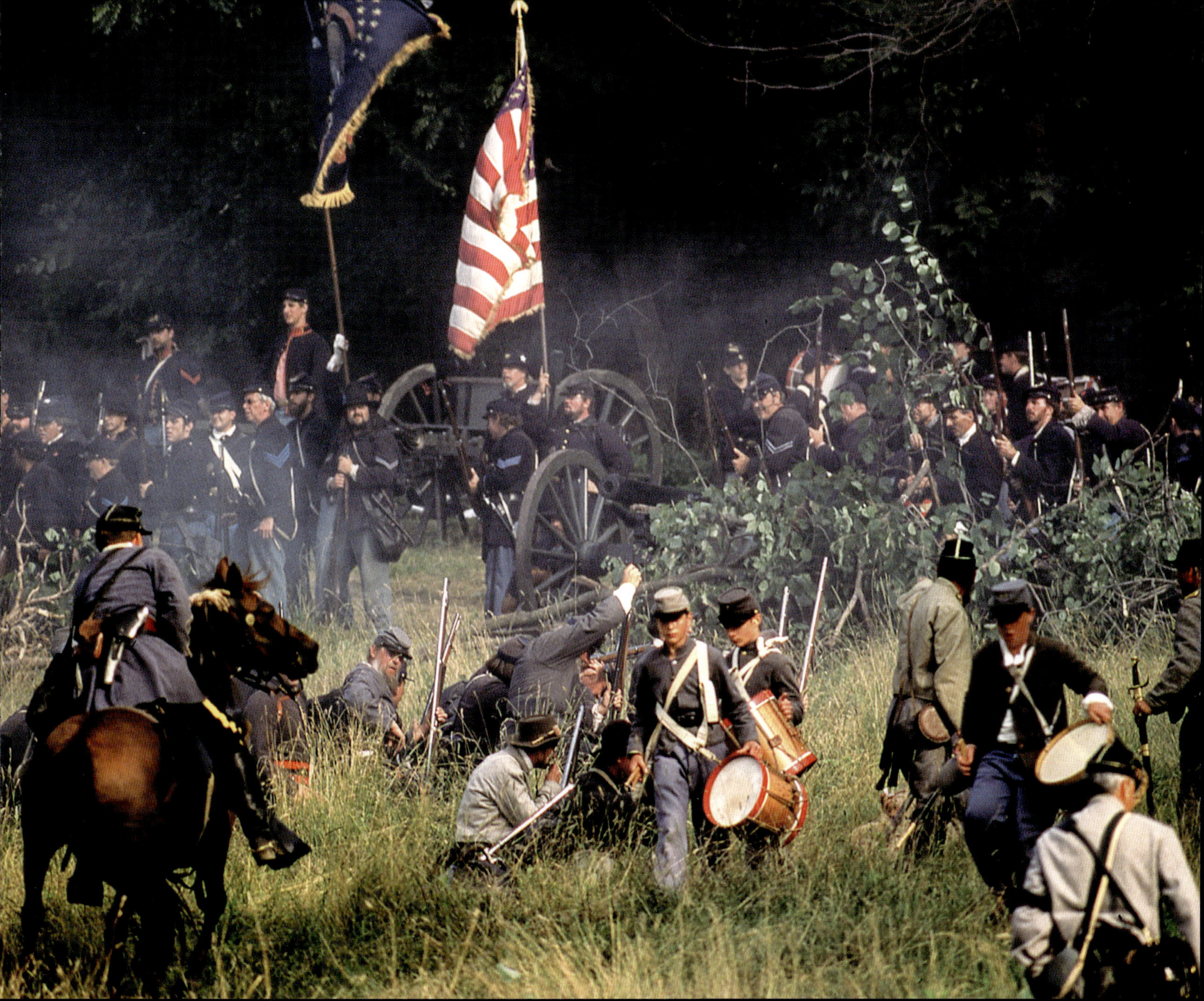

*Above:* Girls play on Amish kick scooters in Lancaster County. Members of the Amish, Mennonite, and Brethren communities settled in eastern Pennsylvania in the early 1700s. These tight-knit Anabaptist Christian communities are known for their plain dress and avoidance of modern conveniences.

*Right:* Landis Valley Village & Farm Museum in Lancaster showcases Pennsylvania German culture, folk traditions, and village life. Brothers Henry and George Landis opened the museum in 1925 to preserve their heritage.

*Facing page:* One of the best ways to enjoy Lancaster County is to follow its winding back roads, where horse-drawn buggy sightings are common.

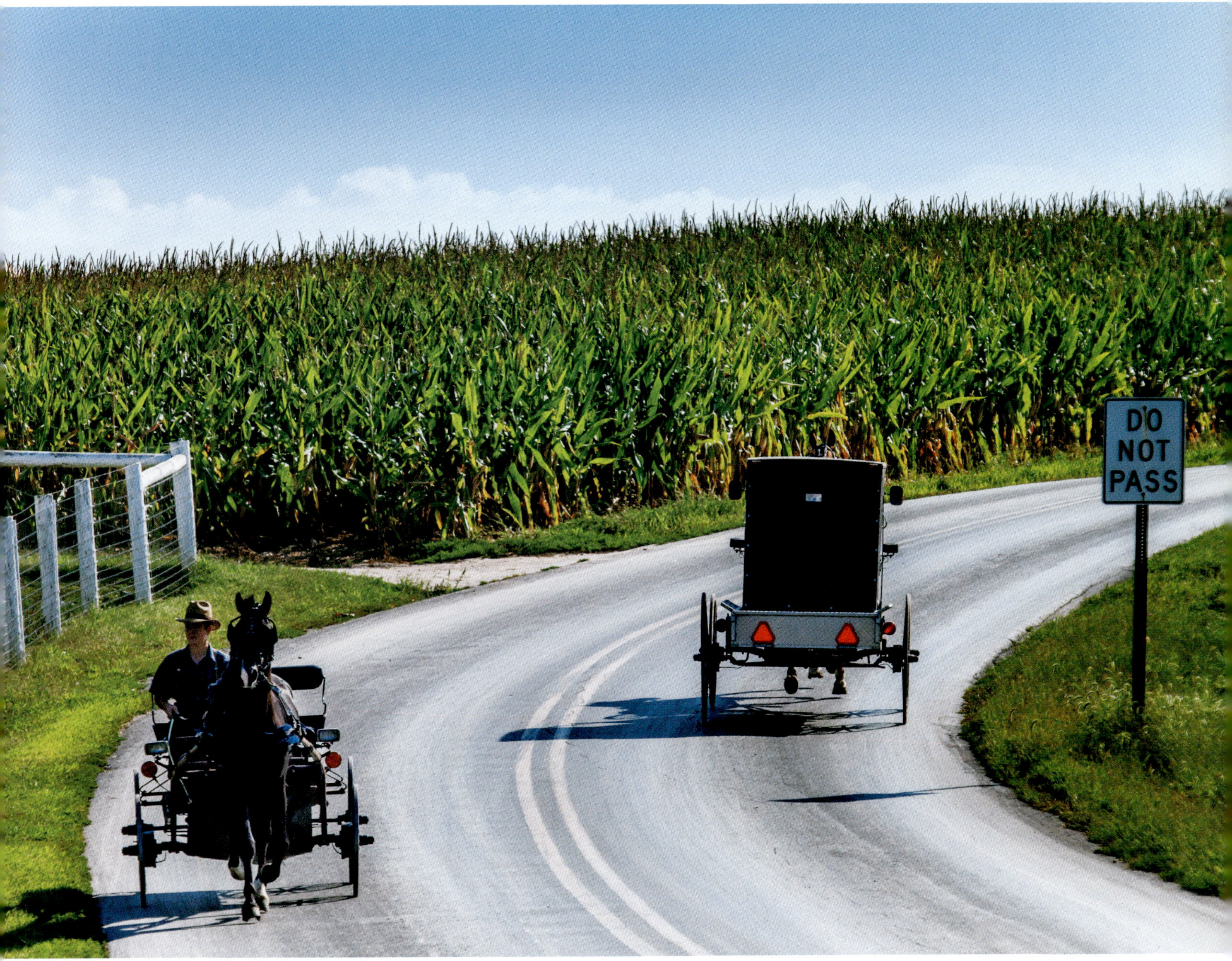
DO
NOT
PASS

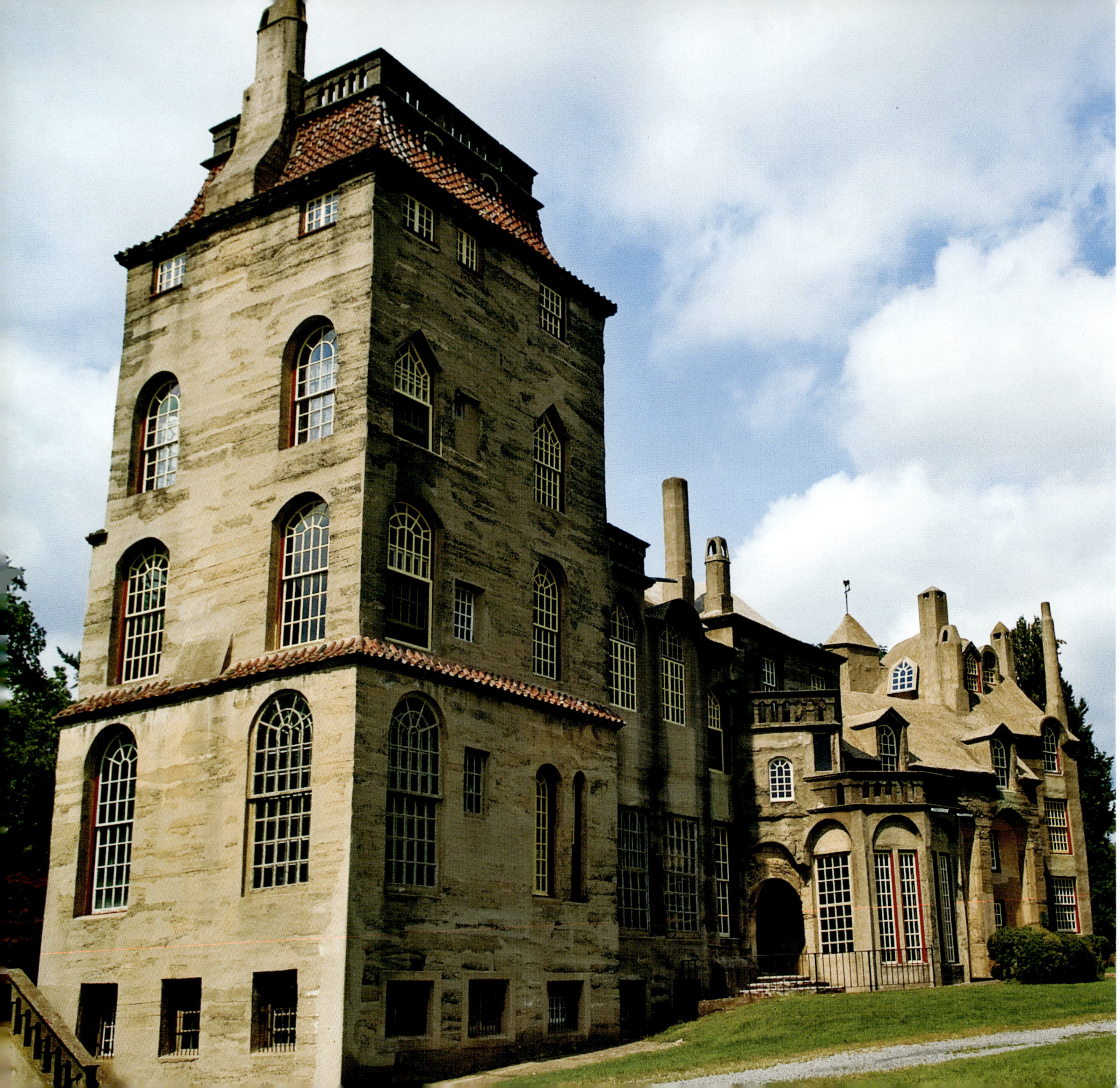

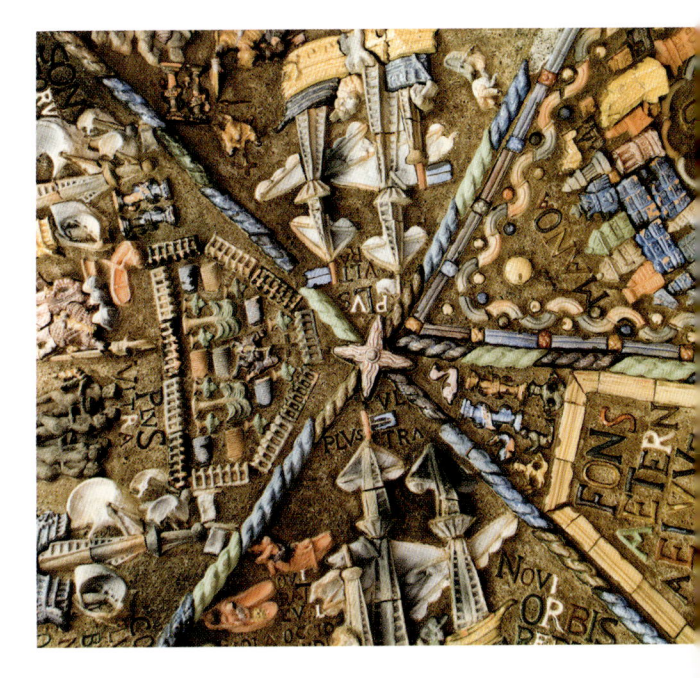

**Above and facing page:** Fonthill Castle is an imposing Doylestown mansion constructed in 1912 by archaeologist, tile-maker, and artist Henry C. Mercer. Handcrafted tiles, both from Mercer's own Moravian Pottery and Tile Works and from abroad, cover nearly every inch of Fonthill's interior.

**Left:** Not far from Fonthill Castle, the Mercer Museum displays Mercer's massive collection across seven rambling stories. Highlights include blacksmith anvils, apple grinders, ox yokes, and firefighting equipment, all from pre-industrial America.

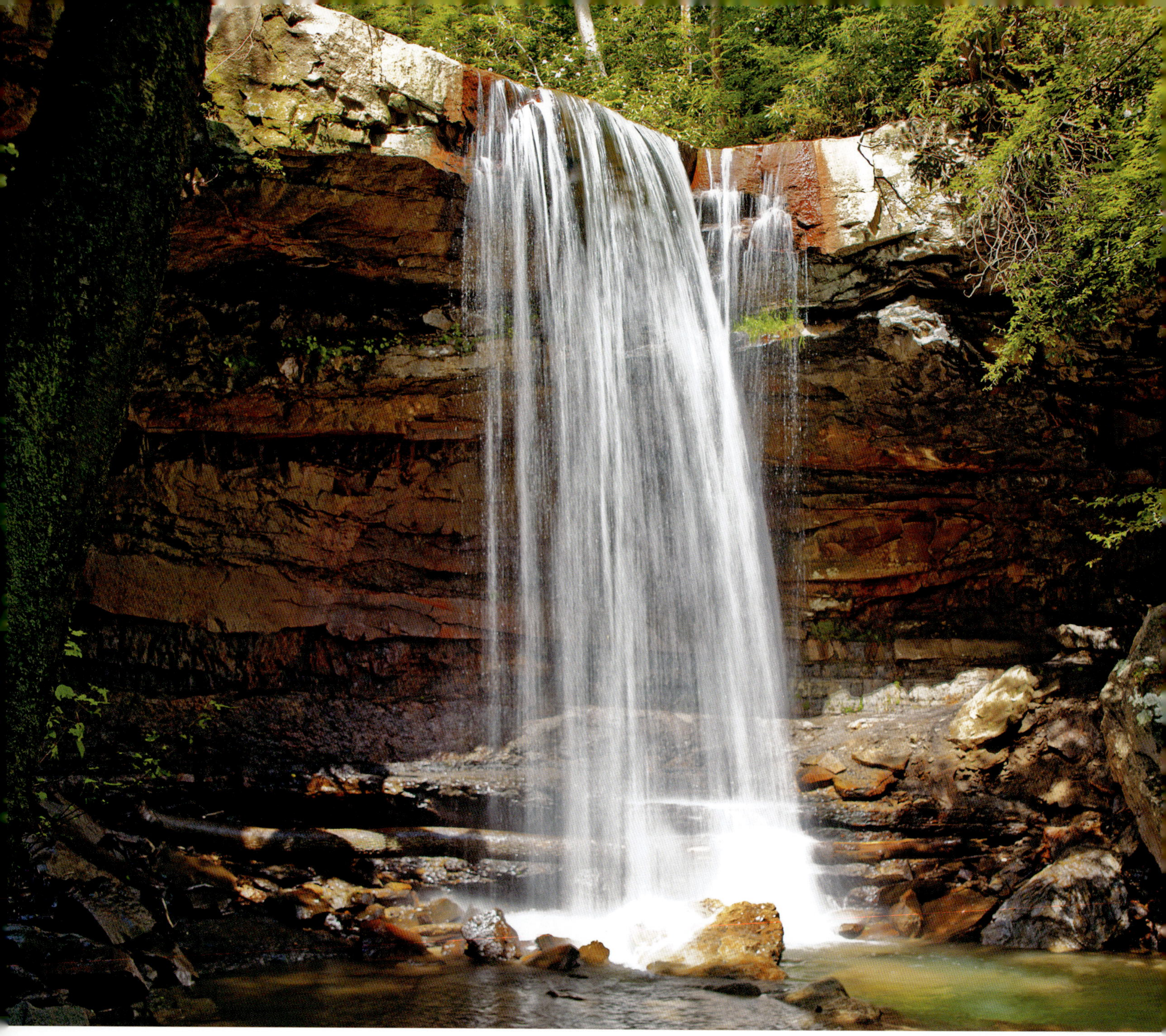

**Above:** See the oil well that launched the modern petroleum industry in Titusville. Drake Well was drilled in 1859, and it is now the focal point of the Drake Well Museum, which also features exhibits on the oil industry, transportation, and firefighting.

**Left:** The white-tailed deer is the official state animal of Pennsylvania. Some 1.5 million whitetails—about three times more than in colonial times—live in the Keystone State.

**Far left:** With its thirty-foot drop and secluded ravine, Cucumber Falls is a popular place to relax in Ohiopyle State Park along the Youghiogheny River in western Pennsylvania's Laurel Highlands.

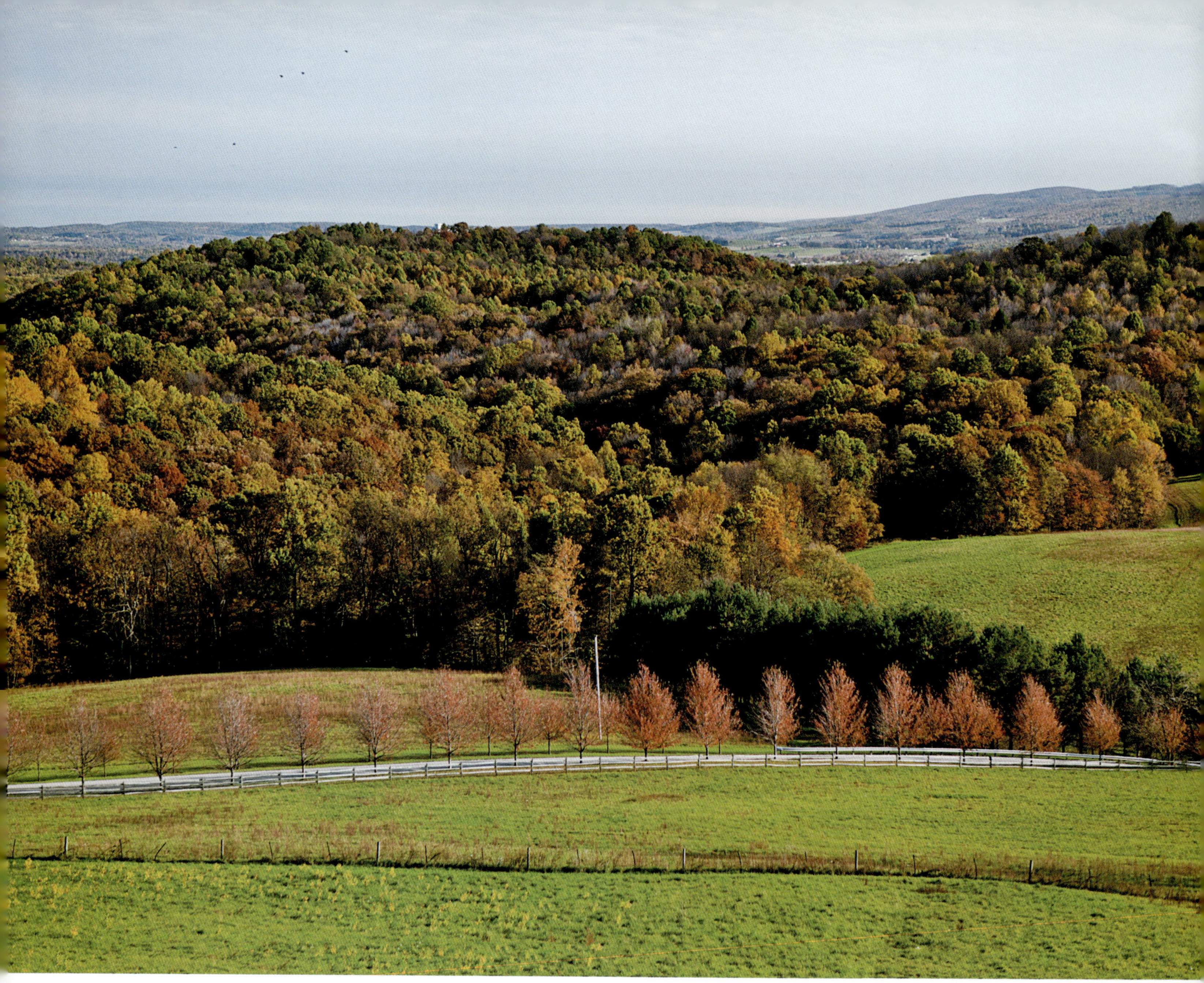

Autumn comes to the Allegheny Mountains, a range of the Appalachians that extends from West Virginia into southeastern Pennsylvania.

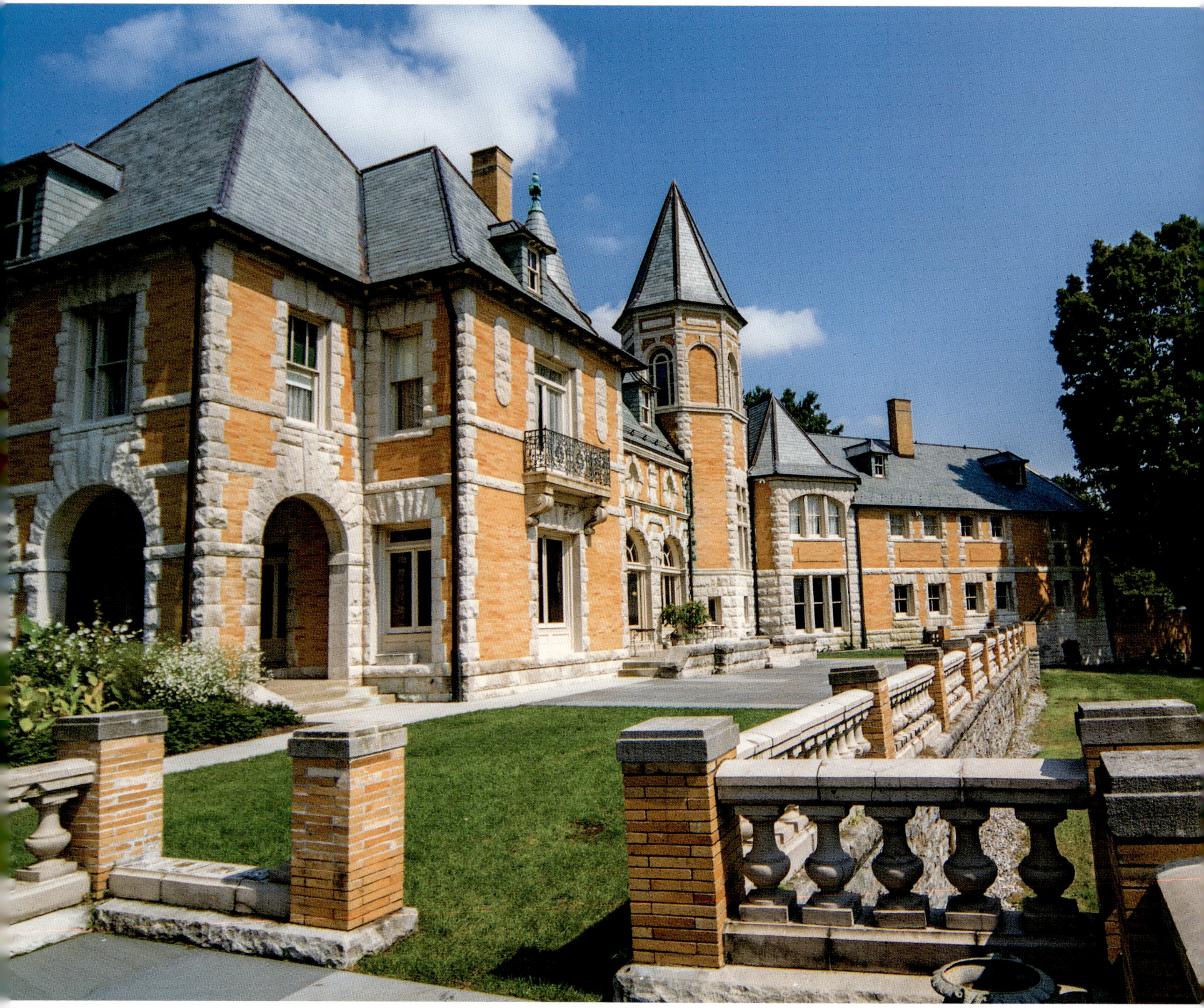

**Left:** Woodmont, an 1892 French Gothic manor house in Gladwyne, serves as the headquarters of the International Peace Mission Movement, a religious group founded in the early 1900s by an evangelist known as Father Divine.

**Below and far left:** Ancient Roman sculptures are part of the classical collection at Glencairn Museum in Bryn Athyn. Once a private home, Glencairn displays Raymond and Mildred Pitcairn's extraordinary collection of religious art, stained glass, sculpture, and other art from a wide variety of cultures.

*Right:* The National Memorial Arch at Valley Forge National Historical Park commemorates the arrival of General George Washington and his troops in 1777. The Continental Army endured the winter of 1777–1778 at Valley Forge, training and preparing for more campaigns despite brutal cold, widespread illness, and lack of supplies.

*Facing page, left:* Now part of Fort Necessity National Battlefield, the Mount Washington Tavern in Farmington served as an important stagecoach stop along the National Road, built in the early 1800s to reach settlements between Cumberland, Maryland, and Vandalia, Illinois.

*Facing page, top right:* A statue inspired by Emmanuel Gottlieb Leutze's 1851 painting *Washington Crossing the Delaware* holds a place of prominence in the town of Washington Crossing. Nearby Washington Crossing State Historic Park marks the location where, in December 1776, Washington and his troops crossed the Delaware to Trenton, New Jersey, to launch a surprise attack.

*Facing page, bottom right:* Created by artist James A. West in 2006, this bronze sculpture, *Point of View*, sits atop Pittsburgh's Mount Washington and depicts a 1770 meeting between Native American chief Guyasuta and George Washington to discuss future settlement along the Ohio River.

51

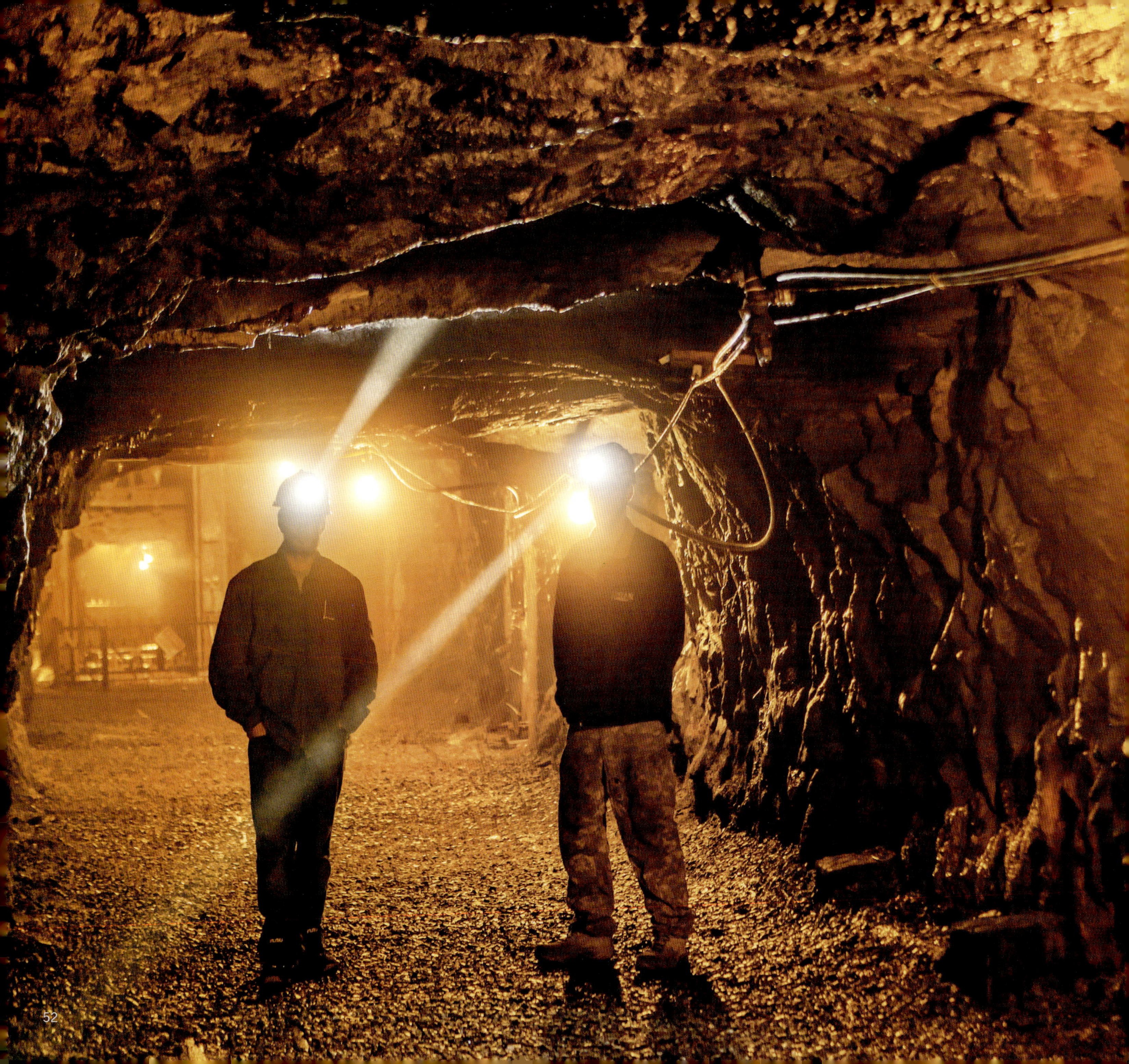

*Above:* The Carrie Furnaces produced iron from 1907 to 1978 and serve as a towering reminder of Pittsburgh's steel industry past. The ninety-two-foot-tall blast furnaces are today part of the Rivers of Steel National Heritage Area.

*Left:* Al Capone's sky-lit cell, his "home" for one year, is part of the regular tours offered at Eastern State Penitentiary in Philadelphia. The prison's wagon-wheel design and stated purpose of reform through isolation served as a model for other nineteenth-century prisons. It closed in 1971 after 142 years of incarcerating criminals.

*Far left:* Visitors ride a train 1,600 feet into the mountainside to see and hear how miners worked at the No. 9 Coal Mine in Lansford, near the town of Jim Thorpe. The mine operated for more than a century before closing in 1972.

***Right:*** Constructed from 1902 to 1906 at a cost of $4.5 million, the Pennsylvania State Capitol blends Greek, Roman, and Victorian architectural influences with tributes to the state's historical achievements. To the top of the dome's statue, Commonwealth, the building measures 272 feet tall.

***Below, left:*** A bronze Confederate soldier helps a wounded Union soldier in Moment of Mercy at the entrance to the National Civil War Museum in Harrisburg.

***Below, right:*** A statue of the commonwealth's founder, William Penn, greets visitors at the State Museum of Pennsylvania in Harrisburg.

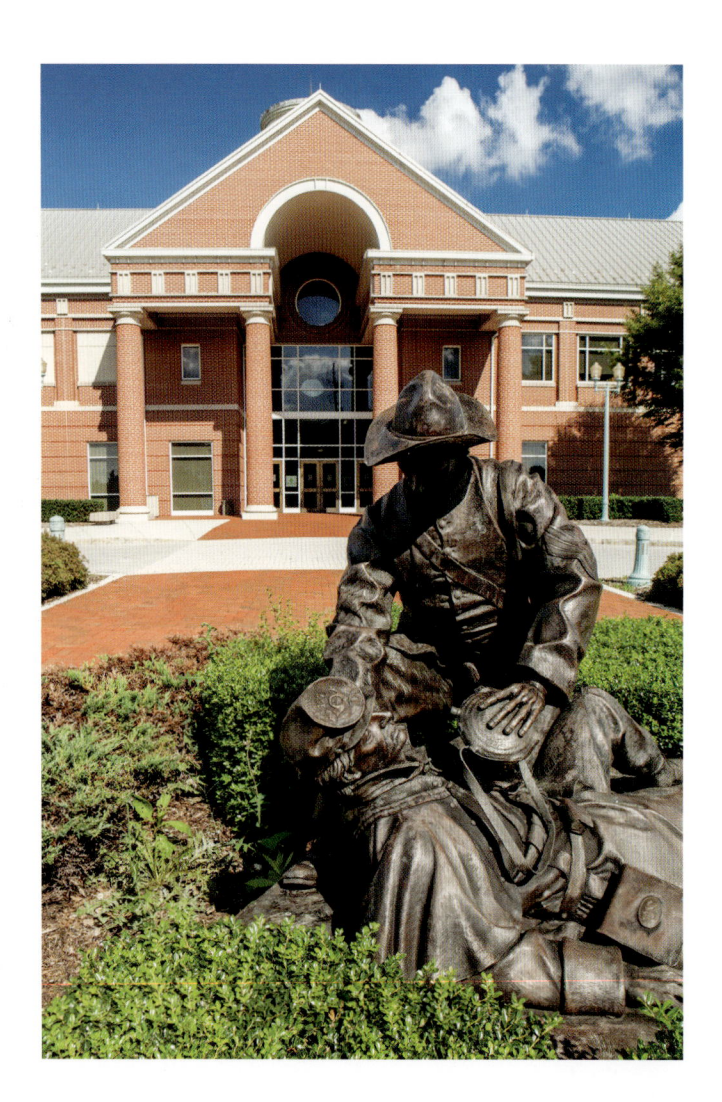

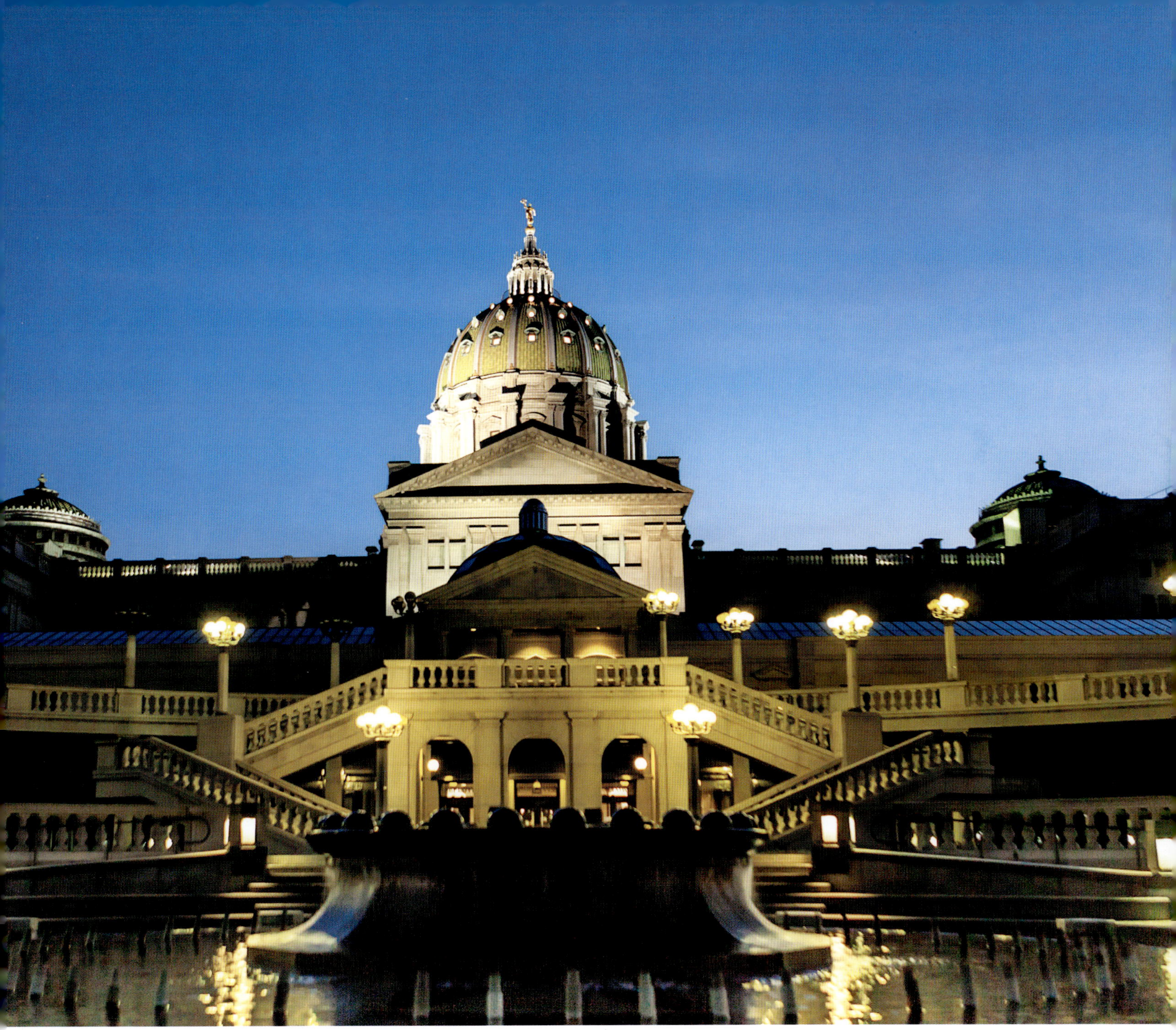

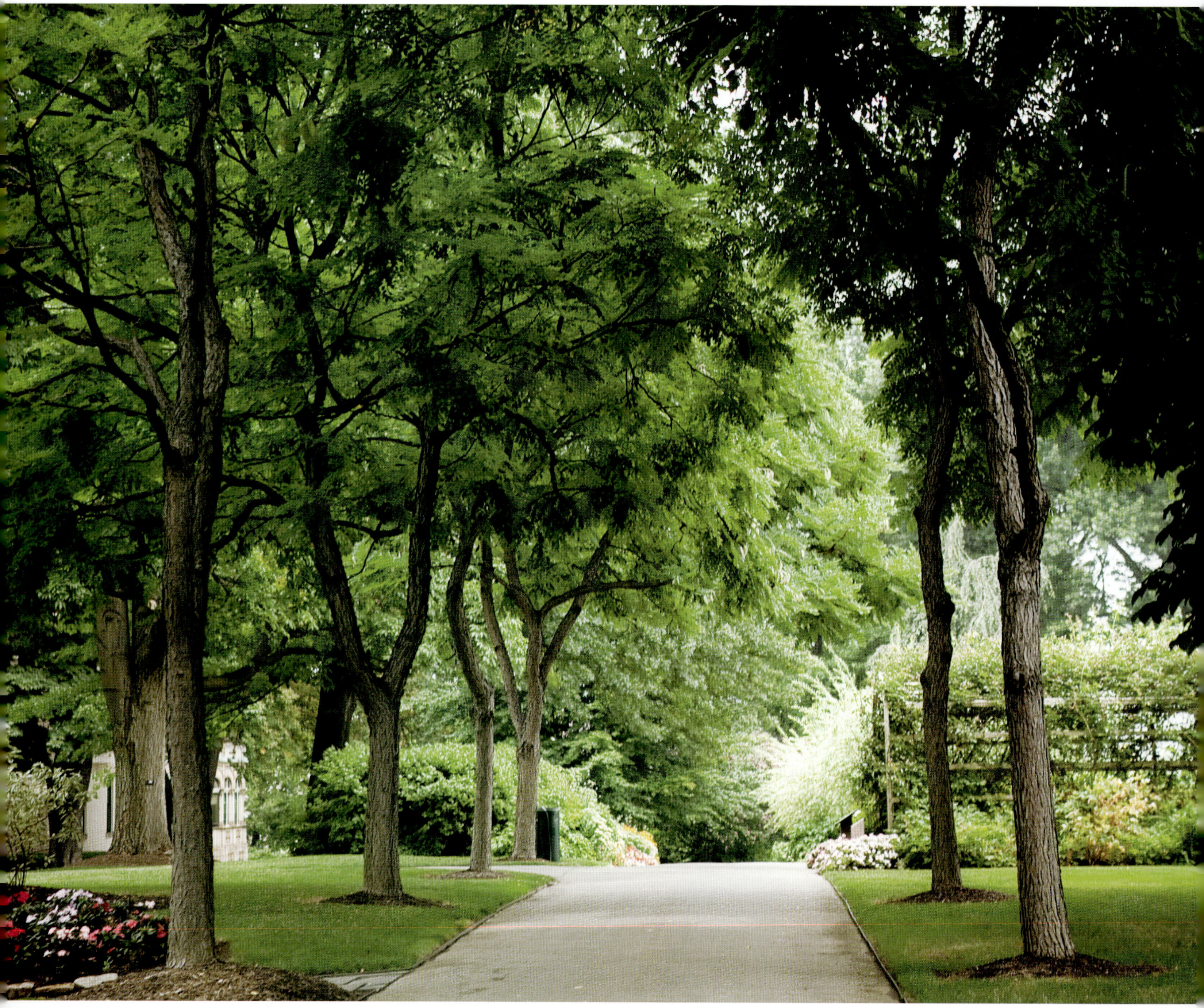

*Facing page:* Pittsburgh's Frick Park covers 644 acres of wooded, rolling hills.

*Left:* A gift from the Heinz family of ketchup fame, the neo-Gothic Heinz Memorial Chapel has hosted religious events, weddings, and lectures on the University of Pittsburgh campus since 1938.

*Below:* Framed by rows of yarrow, the steel and glass Victorian greenhouse at Phipps Conservatory and Botanical Gardens is an architectural centerpiece of Pittsburgh's Schenley Park.

IOVINE'S
PRODUCE
CORNER
BRICK OVEN
FILBERT
IOVINE BROTHERS PRODUCE
HERE COMES

**Left:** The food and produce stalls of Reading Terminal Market sizzle with the flavors and sounds of Philadelphia. Opened in 1893 in an enormous train shed, the Center City landmark's offerings include Pennsylvania delicacies such as Amish shoofly pies, cheesesteaks, and scrapple.

**Below:** Yards Brewing Company turns out British-inspired ales in Philadelphia's Northern Liberties neighborhood.

**Above:** A life-size replica of *Diplodocus carnegii*, one of the longest dinosaurs that ever lived, towers over visitors at the Carnegie Museum of Natural History in Pittsburgh. The dinosaur, the museum, and Pittsburgh's Carnegie Mellon University were all named for billionaire steel mogul and philanthropist Andrew Carnegie.

**Right:** Warm lights promise a cozy stay year-round at Mountaintop Lodge at Lake Naomi. The Pocono Mountains are a prime destination for skiers, golfers, hikers, and shoppers.

**Far right:** The *Pride of the Susquehanna* sternwheeler carries passengers along the scenic Susquehanna River in Harrisburg.

60

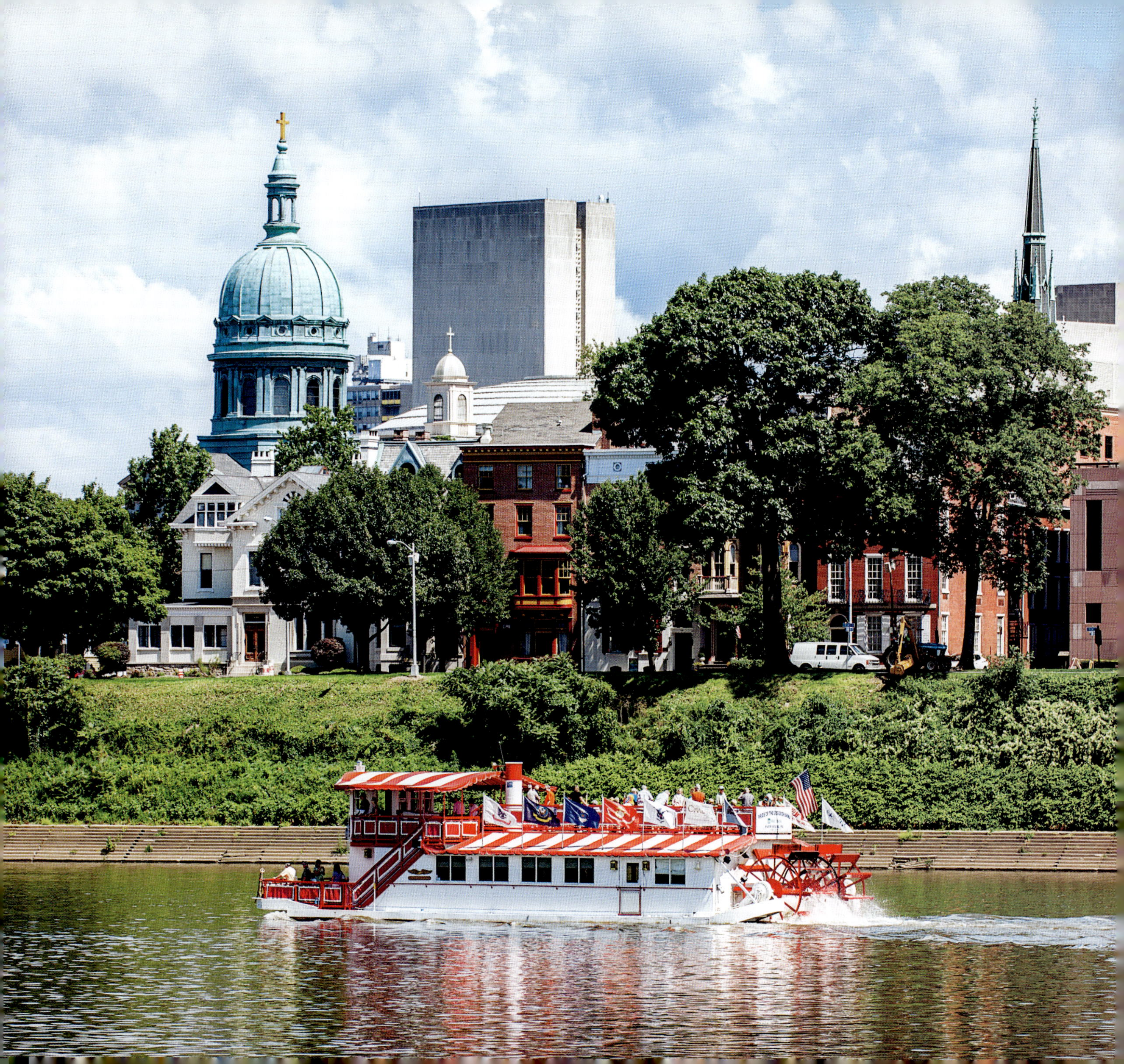

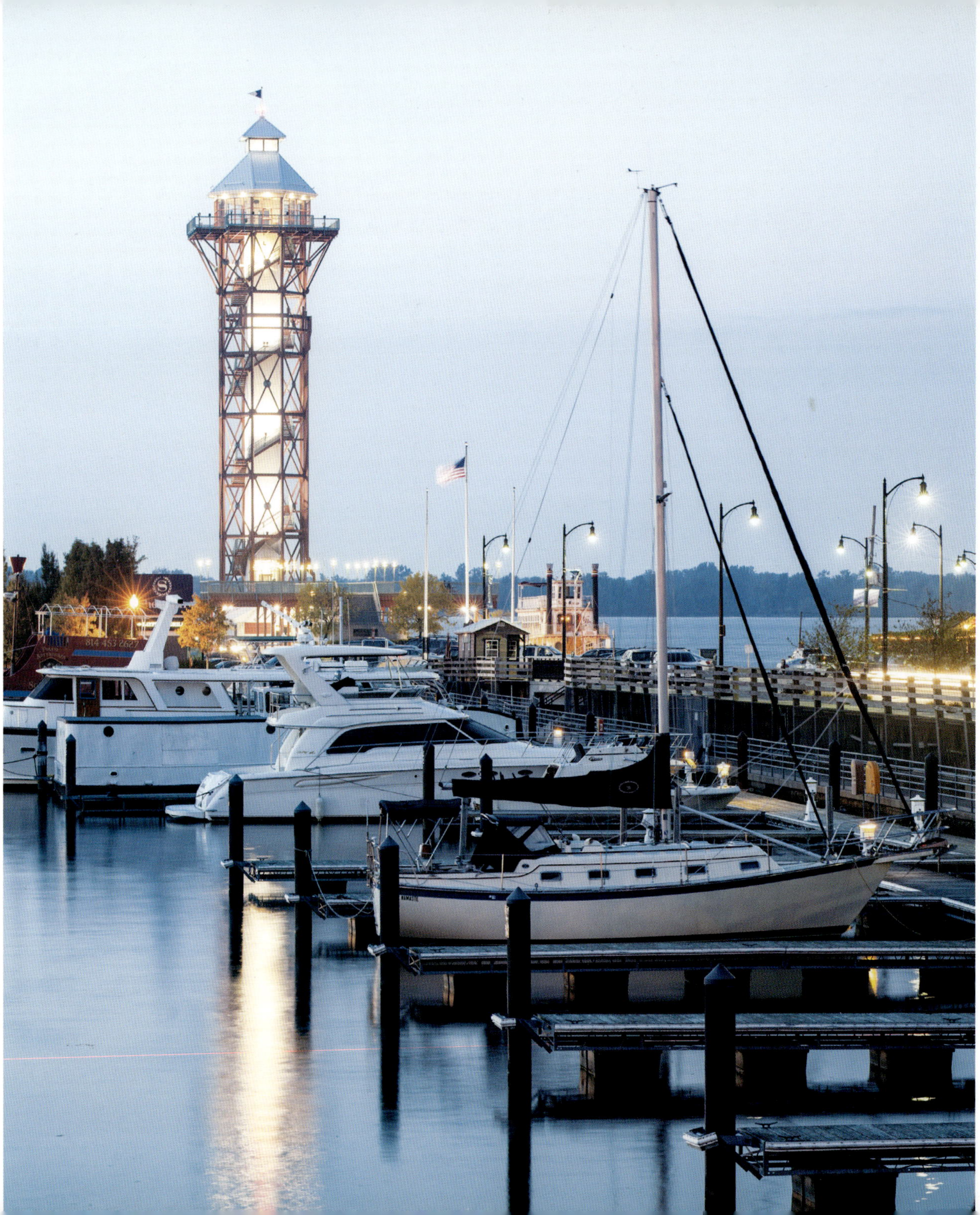

**Left:** The U.S. Brig *Niagara* waits to weigh anchor and set course on Lake Erie. Her home port, Erie, bears the nickname "Flagship City" after this replica of the original flagship *Niagara*, which battled in the War of 1812 under the command of Commodore Oliver Hazard Perry.

**Below and facing page:** Presque Isle State Park in Erie sits on a sandy peninsula that arches into Lake Erie and offers views of its coastline and recreational activities. Observation decks from the 187-foot Bicentennial Tower at Dobbins Landing provide expansive views of Presque Isle, Lake Erie, and downtown Erie, Pennsylvania's only Great Lakes port.

***Facing page:*** A religious community founded by German immigrant Conrad Beissel in the 1730s, the Ephrata Cloister was the center of faith for an estimated 80 celibate worshipers and 200 others who were free to marry. The Cloister faded after Beissel's death in 1768, but living history demonstrators keep its fascinating history alive.

***Right:*** Among the displays at Allentown's America on Wheels museum are modern luxury cars, classic convertibles, antique Mack trucks, and early motorized vehicles.

***Below:*** An Amish farmer tends to his horses at a Lancaster County farmers market.

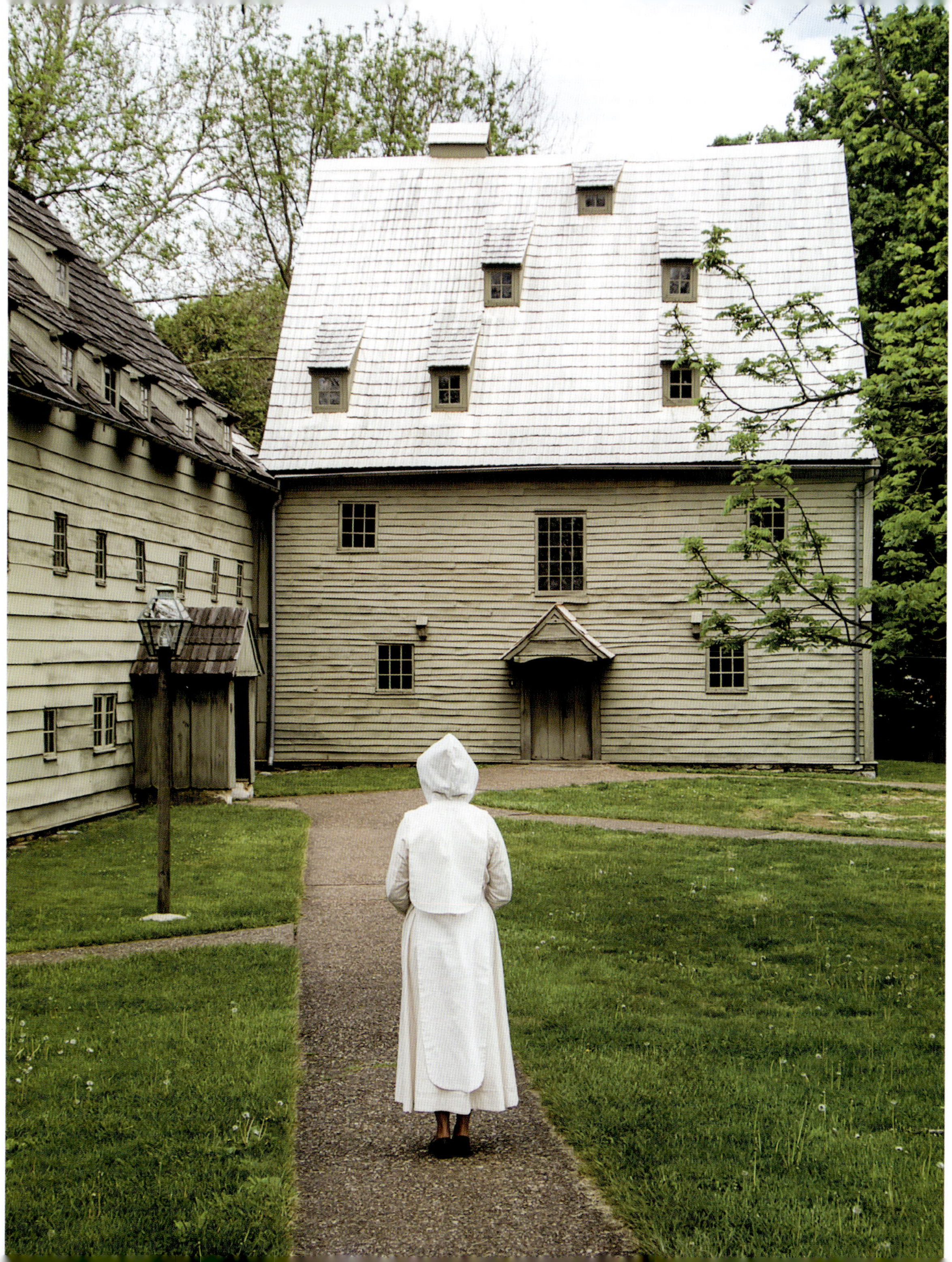

*Facing page:* Each year, more than a million people visit the 2,080-pound bronze Liberty Bell, which heralded America's most important achievements before it was cracked beyond repair in 1846. Although the bell itself has lain silent for decades, its inscription urges visitors to "Proclaim Liberty Throughout All the Land Unto All the Inhabitants thereof."

*Right:* The twenty-foot-tall marble statue of the Benjamin Franklin National Memorial anchors the Franklin Institute's rotunda in Philadelphia. One of the oldest science centers in the country, the museum was created in 1824 to honor the Founding Father and his inventions, which included the lightning rod and bifocals. Today, it is one of the city's most popular attractions.

*Below:* Guided tours of Philadelphia's Independence Hall include a stop at the regal Assembly Room, where the Declaration of Independence was adopted in 1776 and the U.S. Constitution was drafted in 1787. Independence Hall is today part of Independence National Historical Park, along with the Liberty Bell, Benjamin Franklin Museum, a visitor center, and other sites.

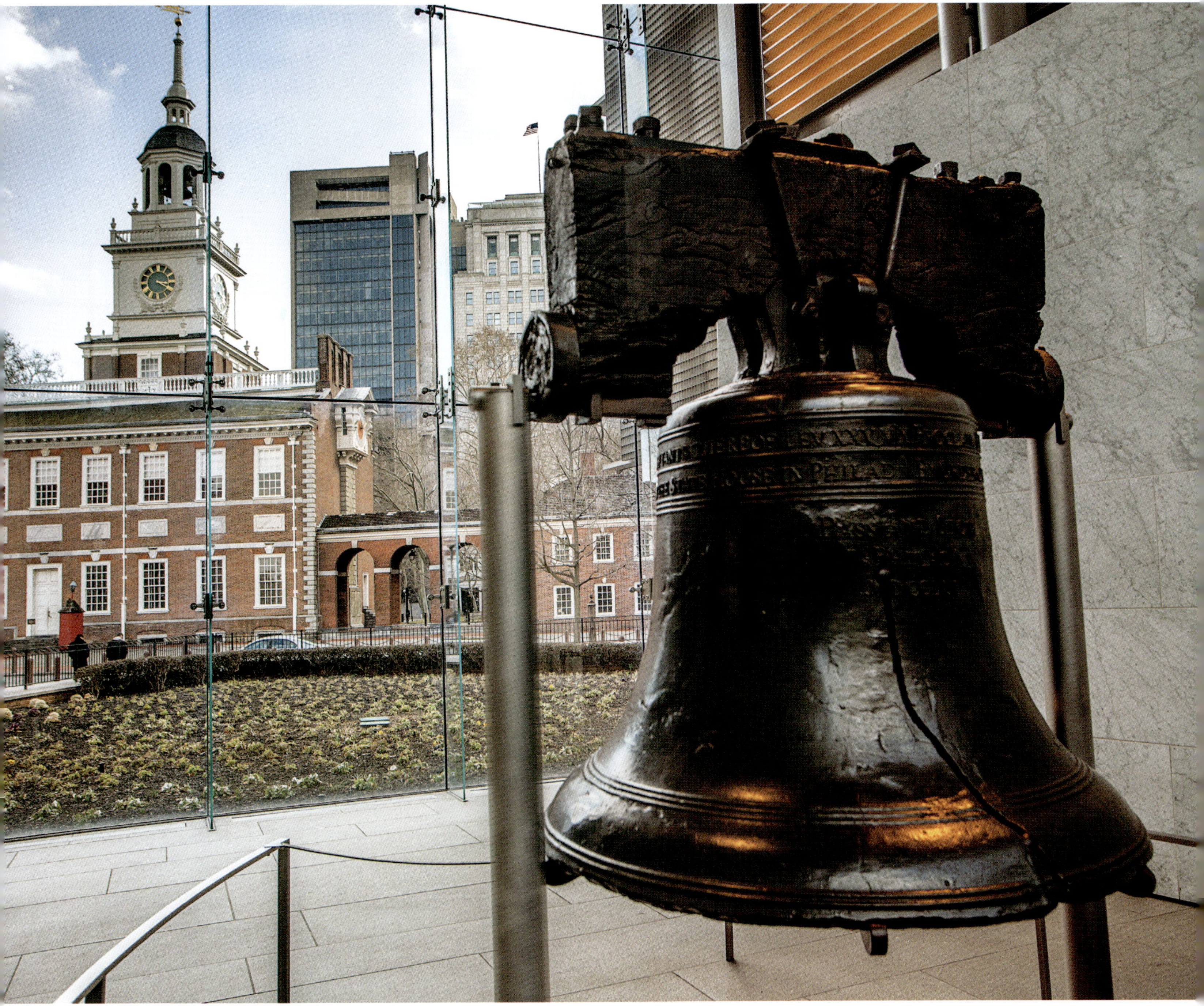

THE
COFFEE
POT
BEDFORD VILLAGE
Settled about 1750, known
then as Raystown. Site of an
early trading post and Fort
Bedford, 1758. Base for Forbes,
Bouquet expeditions. In 1794
Washington here reviewed
forces in Whiskey Rebellion.
PENNSYLVANIA HISTORICAL AND MUSEUM COMMISSION

**Far left:** Built in 1927, the Coffee Pot was once a luncheonette attached to a service station along Lincoln Highway (U.S. Route 30). A fine example of novelty architecture, it now greets visitors at the entrance of the Bedford County Fairgrounds halfway between Harrisburg and Pittsburgh.

**Left:** The Trostletown Bridge, built in 1873 in western Somerset County, is one of nearly 200 authentic covered wooden bridges still standing in Pennsylvania.

**Below:** A bicyclist traverses scenic Route 23 in eastern Lancaster County.

69

Seen from historic Station Square, the Monongahela and Allegheny Rivers reflect Pittsburgh's lighted skyline. The rivers' confluence, which forms the Ohio River, made it a strategic military location. Once the site of the French Fort Duquesne and the British Fort Pitt, it is today Point State Park.

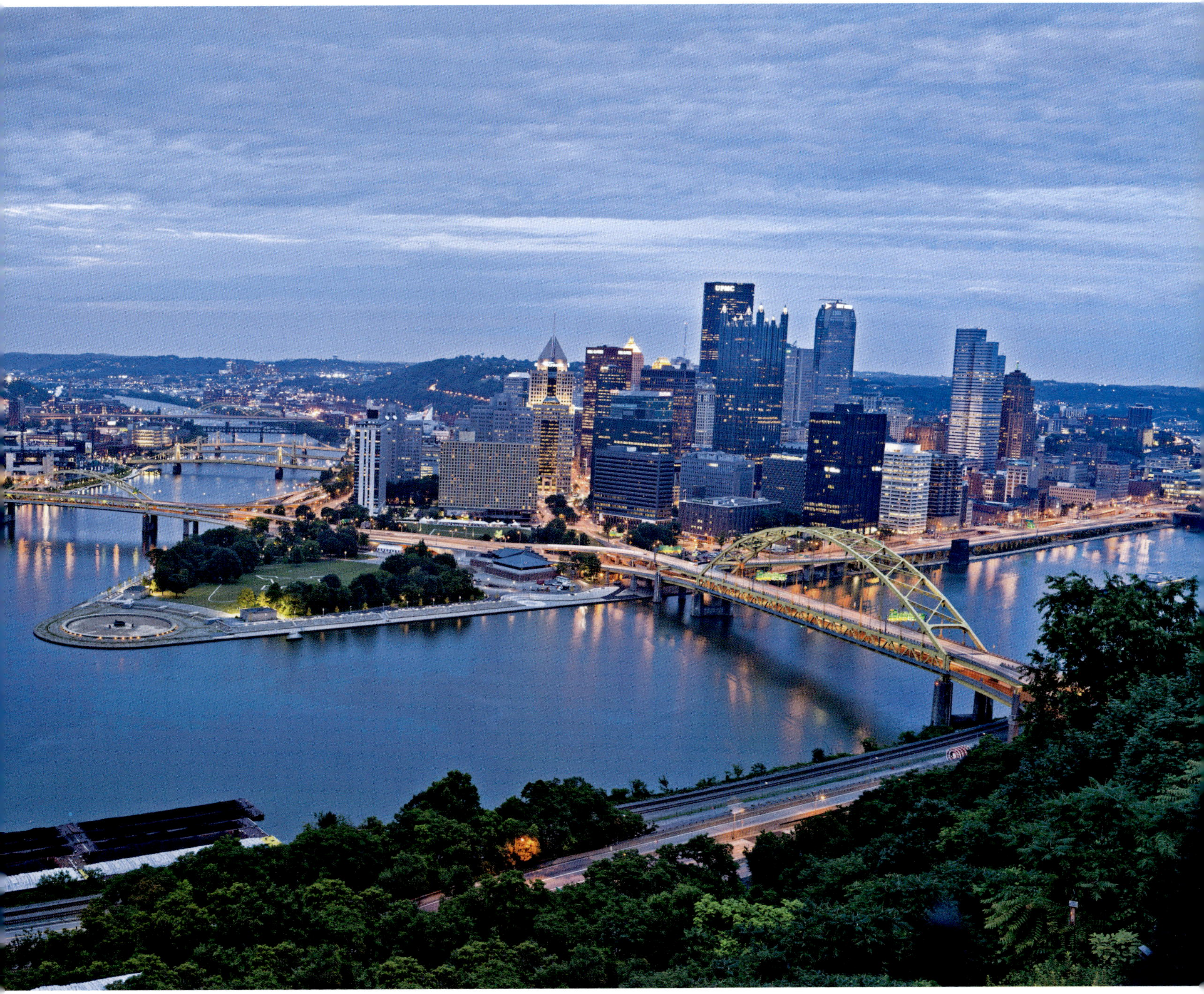
UPMC

*Facing page:* Sixty miles of the Delaware Canal's former towpaths now provide a source of scenic exercise in Delaware Canal State Park.

*Right:* Natural rock ledges and Paupack High Falls flank the Ledges Hotel, a glass factory-turned-hotel in the northern Pocono Mountains town of Hawley.

*Below:* The Harry Packer Mansion, built in 1874 by the founder of the Lehigh Valley Railroad, operates as a bed-and-breakfast on a hillside above the picturesque Pocono Mountains town of Jim Thorpe. The town was known as Mauch Chunk until 1955, when the famous Olympian's widow struck a deal to rename it "Jim Thorpe" and have his remains buried there.

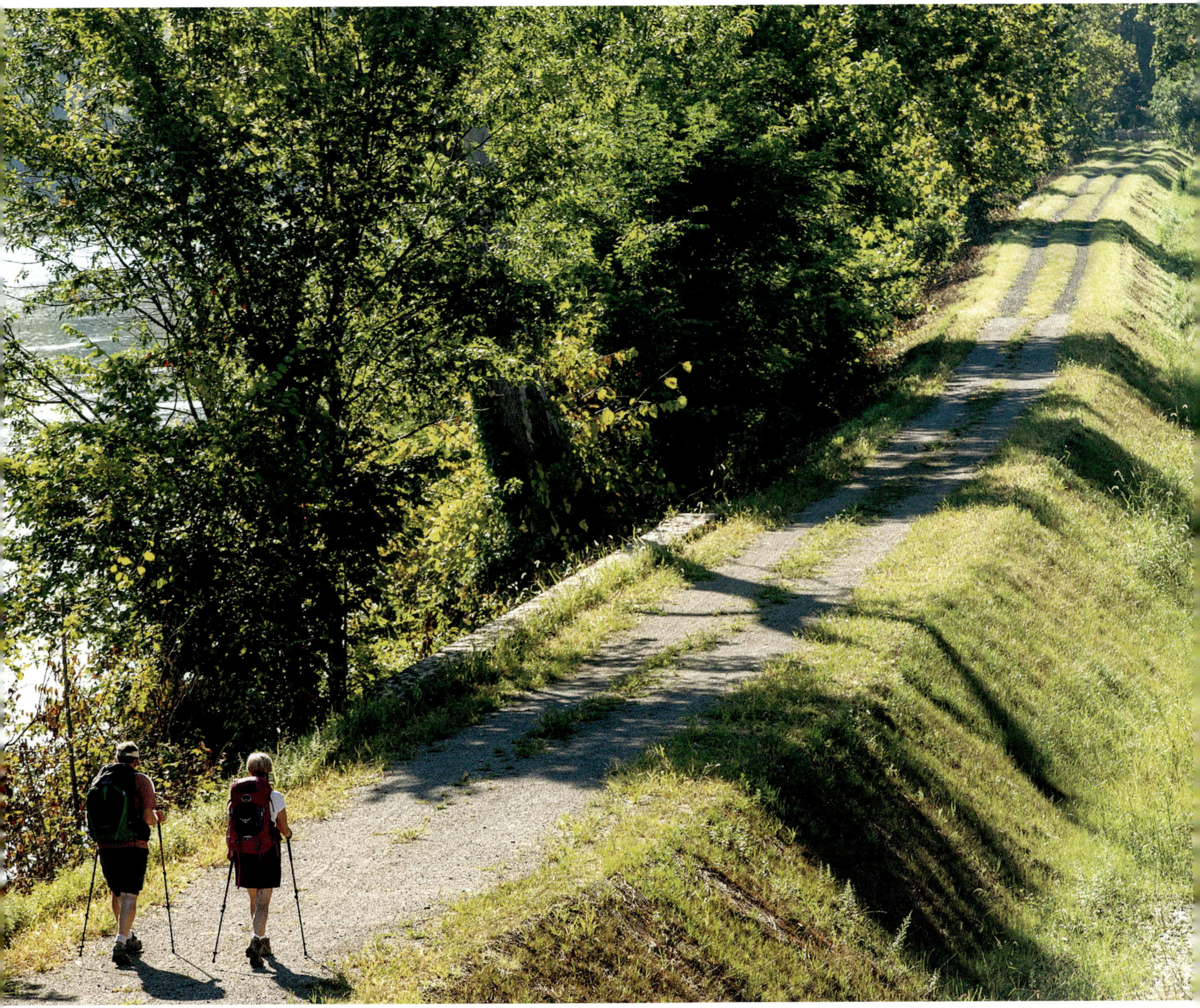

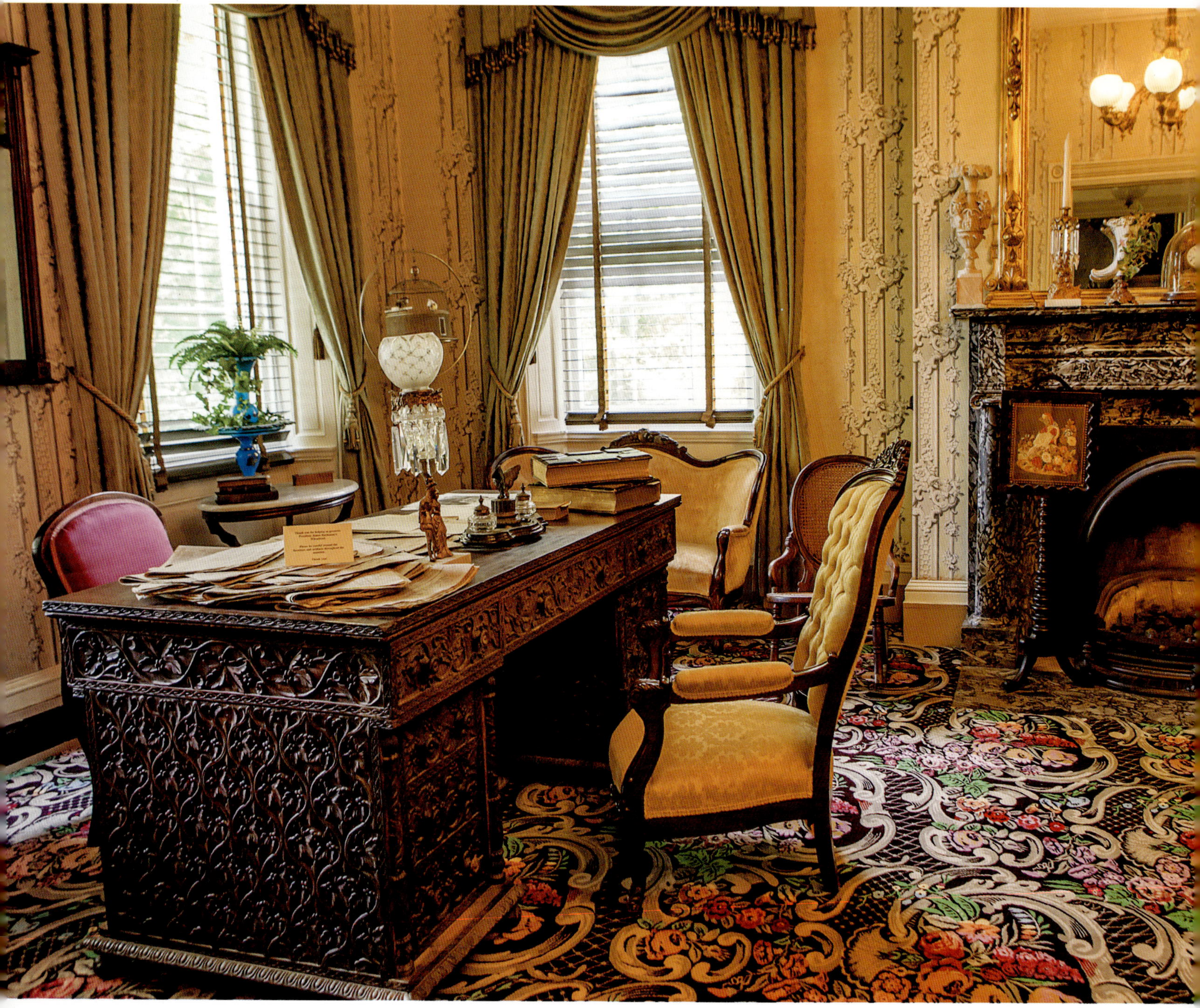

*Far left:* James Buchanan is the only president to hail from Pennsylvania. After leaving office, the fifteenth commander-in-chief lived in Wheatland, this 1828 Federal-style house in Lancaster, for twenty years until his death in 1868.

*Left:* Founded in 1898, Pittsburgh's Kennywood Amusement Park is home to a variety of modern and old-fashioned rides, including a 1927 handcrafted Dentzel Carousel.

*Below:* Stained-glass windows provide a striking backdrop for patrons of the Church Brew Works in Pittsburgh. In 1996, local entrepreneurs turned a deconsecrated 1902 Catholic church into a thriving beer hall brewing handcrafted ales.

75

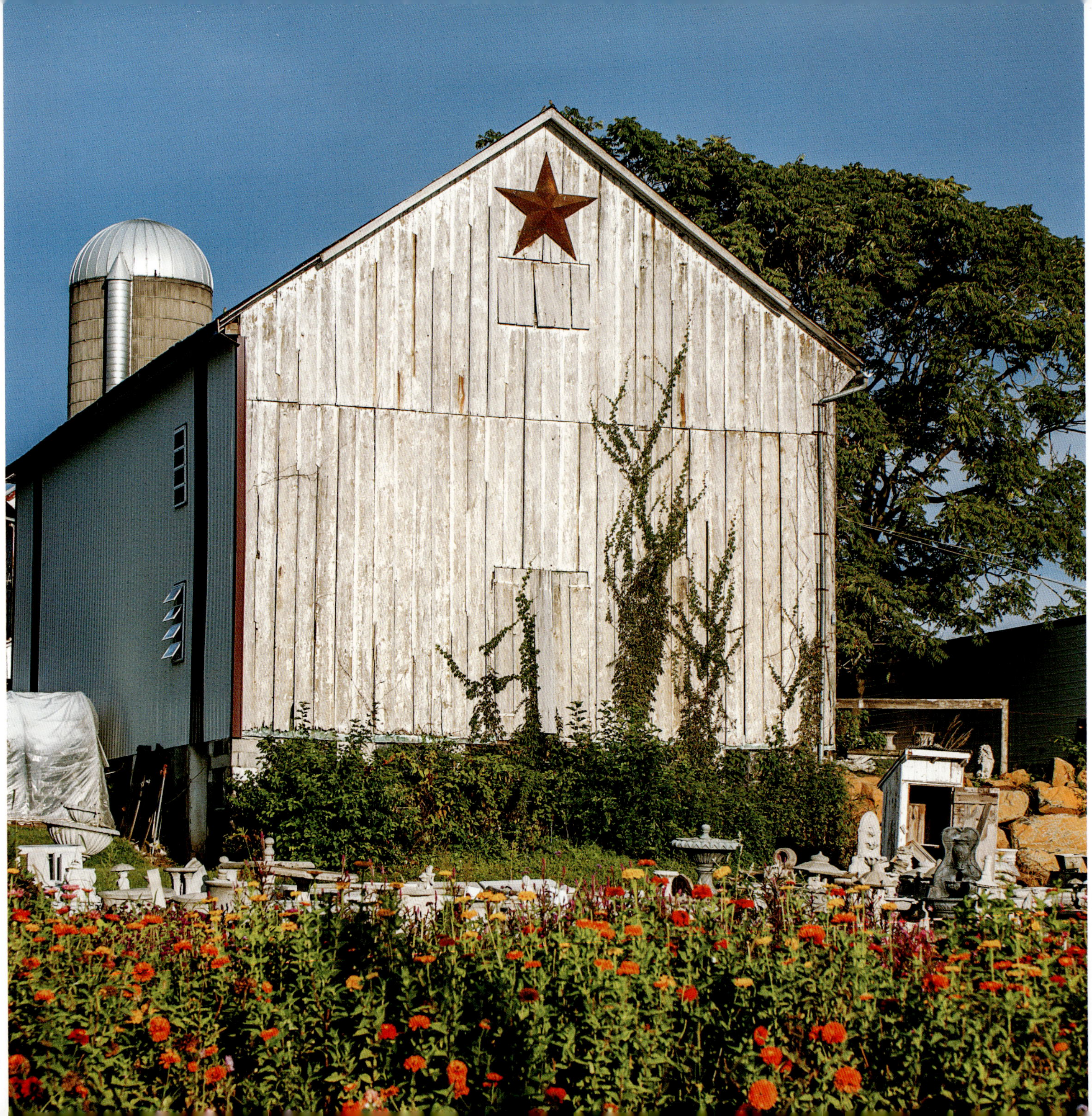

***Above:*** Black Angus cows graze the Eisenhower National Historic Site, a farm outside Gettysburg where Dwight and Mamie Eisenhower often retreated from the demands of the White House.

***Left:*** A young lamb and its mother live on the Colonial Pennsylvania Plantation at Ridley Creek State Park in southeastern Pennsylvania. The working farm serves as an example of rural farm life in eighteenth-century America.

***Facing page:*** Barn stars, locally known as Pennsylvania stars, are good luck folk-art symbols with Pennsylvania Dutch roots. They are a common sight on barns throughout Berks and Lancaster Counties.

*Above:* Permanent exhibits at the State Museum of Pennsylvania in Harrisburg educate residents and visitors about the state's arts, geology, biology, and history. This archaeopteryx fossil was one of the world's earliest birds.

*Right:* Victorian Gothic architecture can be found throughout the campus of the University of Pennsylvania in Philadelphia. Founded in 1740 by a group of Philadelphians that included Benjamin Franklin, UPenn is home to the nation's first medical, law, and business schools.

*Facing page:* The mineral springs and Allegheny Mountain surroundings of the Bedford Springs Resort turned it into one of the country's premier hotels at the turn of the twentieth century. The property underwent a major renovation in 2007, and with its eighteen-hole golf course and historic spa, the resort continues its legacy as a mecca of rejuvenation.

79

PHOTO COURTESY OF DANIELLA NOWITZ

RICHARD NOWITZ, a National Geographic photographer, has forty years of experience in the field and has traveled to more than thirty-five countries across six continents.

Richard's travel photography has won numerous awards, notably Photographer of the Year, the Society of American Travel Writers' highest photography honor, in 1996. He is represented by Corbis Images and National Geographic, and his clients include *National Geographic Traveler*, Insight Guides, Time-Life Books, *Condé Nast Traveler*, and *Endless Vacation*. This book joins more than forty book titles by Nowitz, including *Philadelphia Impressions* from Farcountry Press.

Richard continues to travel and photograph from his home in North Bethesda, Maryland, where he lives with his wife.

See more of Richard's work at www.nowitz.com.